Wright: A Profile

New Poems by Charles Wright

With an Interview

And a Critical Essay by David St. John

Grilled Flowers Press
Profile Editions

Grateful acknowledgement is extended to the following journals in which the poems in this Profile first appeared: **Antaeus, Field, Missouri Review, New England Review, The New Yorker, Paris Review, Quarterly West,** and **Seneca Review.**

"Homage to Paul Cezanne" © 1977 **The New Yorker Magazine, Inc.**

Section I of David St. John's "The Poetry of Charles Wright" first appeared in **Seneca Review.**

"Self-Portrait" by Charles Wright first appeared in **Seneca Review.**

"Holy Thursday," "Self-Portrait," and "Virginia Reel" Copyright © 1978 by **Antaeus.** Reprinted by permission.

The publication of this Grilled Flowers Profile Edition was made possible by a generous grant from the the National Endowment for the Arts, a federal agency, in Washington, D.C. Many thanks also to the Arizona Commission on the Arts and Humanities for their support of this project.

The frontispiece, Paul Cezanne's drawing "Le Moulin a platre, 1889-92," is from the Collection of Mr. and Mrs. Paul Mellon, Upperville, Virginia.

Photograph of the poet, page 68, by Holly Wright

ISBN 0-931238-06-4
ISBN 0-931238-07-2 (Signed and lettered)

Printed in the United States of America for:

Grilled Flowers Press
Frank Graziano, Editor
Post Office Box 809
Iowa City, Iowa 52240

CONTENTS

Self-Portrait

Marostica, Val di Ser. Bassano del Grappa.
Madonna del Ortolo. San Giorgio, arcade stone.
The foothills above the Piave.

Places and things that caught my eye, walk
in Italy. Oxford, peat catalogues, some 20-odd
                                            years ago.

San Zeno and Caffe Dante. Catullus' seat.
Lake Garda. The Adige at Ponte Pietra
— I still haunt there, a shimmer across the bridge on hot days,
the dust, for a little while, lying lightly along my sleeve.
Piazza Erbe, the 12 Apostles...

Opus restored of John Keats
The winter night comes down, its black habit starless
                                            and edged with ice,
The breath of those who are rising from the dead.

Dino Campana, Arthur Rimbaud
Hart Crane and Emily Dickinson. The Black Chateau

Poems (I)

HOMAGE TO PAUL CEZANNE

At night, in the fish-light of the moon, the dead wear our
    white shirts
To stay warm, and litter the fields.
We pick them up in the mornings, dewy pieces of paper and
    scraps of cloth.

Like us, they refract themselves. Like us,
They keep on saying the same thing, trying to get it
    right.
Like us, the water unsettles their names.

Sometimes they lie like leaves in their little arks, and curl
    up at the edges.

Sometimes they come inside, wearing our shoes, and walk
From mirror to mirror.
Or lie in our beds with their gloves off
And touch our bodies. Or talk
In a corner. Or wait like envelopes on a desk.

They reach up from the ice plant.
They shuttle their messengers through the oat grass.
Their answers rise like rust on the stalks and the spidery
    leaves.

We rub them off our hands.

Each year the dead grow less dead, and nudge
Close to the surface of all things.
They start to remember the silence that brought them there.
They start to recount the gain in their soiled hands.

Their glasses let loose, and grain by grain return to the
        river bank
They point to their favorite words
Growing around them, revealed as themselves for the
        first time:
They stand close to the meanings and take them in.

They stand there, vague and without pain,
Under their fingernails an unreturnable dirt.
They stand there and it comes back,
The music of everything, syllable after syllable

Out of the burning chair, out of the beings of light.
It all comes back.
And what they repeat to themselves, and what they
        repeat to themselves,
Is the song that our fathers sing.

In steeps and sighs,
The ocean explains itself, backing and filling
What spaces it can't avoid, spaces
In black shoes, their hands clasped, their eyes teared at
      the edges:
We watch from the high hillside,
The ocean swelling and flattening, the spaces
Filling and emptying, horizon blade
Flashing the early afternoon sun.

The dead are constant in
The white lips of the sea.
Over and over, through clenched teeth, they tell
Their story, the story each knows by heart:
Remember me, speak my name.
When the moon tugs at my sleeve,
When the body of water is raised and becomes the body of
      light,
Remember me, speak my name.

The dead are a cadmium blue.
We spread them with palette knives in broad blocks and
    planes.

We layer them stroke by stroke
In steps and ascending mass, in verticals raised from the
    earth.

We choose, and layer them in,
Blue and a blue and a breath,

Circle and smudge, cross-beak and button hook,
We layer them in. We squint hard and terrace them line
    by line.

And so we are come between, and cry out,
And stare up at the sky and its cloudy panes,

And finger the cypress twists.
The dead understand all this, and keep in touch,

Rustle of hand to hand in the lemon trees,
Flags, and the great sifts of anger

To powder and nothingness.
The dead are a cadmium blue, and they understand.

The dead are with us to stay.
Their shadows rock in the back yard, so pure, so black,
Between the oak tree and the porch.

Over our heads they're huge in the night sky.
In the tall grass they turn with the zodiac.
Under our feet they're white with the snows of a
      thousand years.

They carry their colored threads and baskets of silk
To mend our clothes, making us look right,
Altering, stitching, replacing a button, closing a tear.
They lie like tucks in our loose sleeves, they hold us
      together.

They blow the last leaves away.
They slide like an overflow into the river of heaven.
Everywhere they are flying.

The dead are a sleight and a fade
We fall for, like flowering plums, like white coins from the
      rain.
Their sighs are gaps in the wind.

The dead are waiting for us in our rooms,
Little globules of light
In one of the far corners, and close to the ceiling,
    hovering, thinking our thoughts.

Often they'll reach a hand down,
Or offer a word, and ease us out of our bodies to join
    them in theirs.
We look back at our other selves on the bed.

We look back and we don't care and we go.

And thus we become what we've longed for,
                                past tense and otherwise,
A BB, a disc of light,
                    song without words.
And refer to ourselves
In the third person, seeing that other arm
Still raised from the bed, fingers like licks and flames in
    the boned air.

Only to hear that it's not time.
Only to hear that we must re-enter and lie still, our arms
    at rest at our sides,
The voices rising around us like mist

And dew, *it's all right, it's all right, it's all right...*

The dead fall around us like rain.
They come down from the last clouds in the late light for
        the last time
And slip through the sod.

They lean uphill and face north.
                              Like grass,
They bend toward the sea, they break toward the setting
        sun.

We filigree and we baste.
But what do the dead care for the fringe of words,
Safe in their suits of milk?
What do they care for the honk and flash of a new style?

And who is to say if the inch of snow in our hearts
Is rectitude enough?

Spring picks the locks of the wind.
High in the night sky the mirror is hauled up and
        unsheeted.
In it we twist like stars.

Ahead of us, through the dark, the dead
Are beating their drums and stirring the yellow leaves.

We're out here, our feet in the soil, our heads craned up at
　　　the sky,
The stars streaming and bursting behind the trees.

At dawn, as the clouds gather, we watch
The mountain glide from the east on the valley floor,
Coming together in starts and jumps.
Behind their curtain, the bears
Amble across the heavens, serene as black coffee...

Whose unction can intercede for the dead?
Whose tongue is toothless enough to speak their piece?

What we are given in dreams we write as blue paint,
Or messages to the clouds.
At evening we wait for the rain to fall and the sky to
　　　clear.
Our words are words for the clay, uttered in undertones,
Our gestures salve for the wind.

We sit out on the earth and stretch our limbs,
Hoarding the little mounds of sorrow laid up in our
　　　hearts.

Poems (II)

SELF-PORTRAIT

Someday they'll find me out, and my lavish hands,
Full moon at my back, fog groping the gone horizon, the
      edge
Of the continent scored in yellow, expectant lights,
White shoulders of surf, a wolf-colored sand,
The ashes and bits of char that will clear my name.

Till then, I'll hum to myself and settle the whereabouts.
Jade plants and oleander float in a shine.
The leaves of the pepper tree turn green.
My features are sketched with black ink in a slow drag
      through the sky,
Waiting to be filled in.

Hand that lifted me once, lift me again,
Sort me and flesh me out, fix my eyes.
From the mulch and the undergrowth, protect me and
      pass me on.
From my own words and my certainties,
From the rose and the easy cheek, deliver me, pass me on.

MOUNT CARIBOU AT NIGHT

Just north of the Yaak River, one man sits bolt up-right,
A little bonnet of dirt and bunch grass above his head:
Northwestern Montana is hard relief,
And harder still the lying down and the rising up...

I speak to the others there, lodged in their stone wedges,
    the blocks
And slashes that vein the ground, and tell them that
    Walter Smoot,
Starched and at ease in his bony duds
Under the tamaracks, still holds the nightfall between his
    knees.

Work stars, drop by inveterate drop, begin
Cassiopeia's sails and electric paste
Across the sky. And down
Toward the cadmium waters that carry them back to the
    dawn,

They squeeze out Andromeda and the Whale,
Everything on the move, everything flowing and folding
    back
And starting again,
Star-slick, the flaking and crusting duff at my feet,

Smoot and Runyan and August Binder
Still in the black pulse of the earth, cloud-gouache
Over the tree-line, Mount Caribou
Massive and on the rise and taking it in. And taking it
    back

To the future we occupied, and will wake to again,
      ourselves
And our children's children snug in our monk's robes,
Pushing the cauly hoods back, ready to walk out
Into the same night and the meadow grass, in step and
      on time...

SELF-PORTRAIT

Charles on the Trevisan, night bridge
To the crystal, infinite alphabet of his past.
Charles on the San Trovaso, earmarked,
Holding the pages of a thrown-away book, dinghy the
    color of honey
Under the pine boughs, the water east-flowing.

The wind will edit him soon enough,
And squander his broken chords
                  in tiny striations above the air,
No slatch in the undertow.
The sunlight will bear him out,
Giving him breathing room, and a place to lie.

And why not? The reindeer still file through the
    bronchial trees,
Holding their heads high.
The mosses still turn, the broomstraws flash on and off.
Inside, in the crosslight, and St. Jerome
And his creatures...St. Augustine, striking the words out...

HOLY THURSDAY

Begins with the *ooo ooo* of a mourning dove
In the pepper tree, crack
Of blue and a flayed light on the hills,
Myself past the pumpkin blooms and out in the disced
    field,
Blake's children still hunched in sleep, dollops
Of bad dreams and an afterlife.
Canticles rise in spate from the bleeding heart.
Cathedrals assemble and disappear in the water beads.
I scuff at the slick adobe, one eye
On the stalk and one on the aftermath.

There's always a time for rust,
For looking down at the earth and its lateral chains.
There's always a time for the grass, teeming
Its little four-cornered purple flowers,
                         tricked out in an oozy shine.
There's always a time for the dirt.
Reprieve, reprieve, the flies drone, their wings
Increasingly incandescent above the corn silk.
No answer from anything, four crows
On a eucalyptus limb, speaking in tongues.
No answer for them, either.

It's noon in the medlar tree, the sun
Sifting its glitter across the powdery stems.
It doesn't believe in God
And still is absolved.
It doesn't believe in God
And seems to get by, going from here to there.
Butterflies blow like pieces of half-burned construction
       paper over the sweet weeds
And take what is given them.
Some hummer is luckier
Downwind, and smells blood, and seeks me out.

The afternoon hangs by a leaf.
The vines are a green complaint
From the slaking adobe dust. I settle and stand back.
The hawk realigns herself.
Splatter of mockingbird notes, a brief trill from the jay.
The fog starts in, breaking its various tufts loose.
Everything smudges and glows,
Cactus, the mustard plants and the corn,
Through the white reaches of 4 o'clock...
There's always a time for words.

Surf sounds in the palm tree,
Susurrations, the wind
                            making a big move from the west,
The children asleep again, their second selves
Beginning to stir, the moon
Lop-sided, sliding their ladder down.
From under the billowing dead, from their wet hands and
        a saving grace,
The children begin to move, an angle of phosphorescence
Along the ridge line.
                            Angels
Are counting cadence, their skeletal songs
What the hymns say, the first page and the last.

SELF-PORTRAIT

The pictures in the air have few visitors.

Sun drops past tie-post in the east shallows,
Moon rises to camera range. Over the zodiac,
The numbers and definitions arc,
Hiwassee at low tide, my brother one step up the cleared
      slope.

Winter on top of the Matterhorn,
Sun-goggled, standing the way our father stood, hands
      half in his pockets.
Behind him, the summer Alps
Fall down and away, little hillocks of white on the noon
      sky
Hiding their crosses, keeping the story straight.

Like Munch, I languish, my left cheek in my left palm,
Omniscient above the bay,
Checking the evidence, the postcards and the
      photographs,
O'Grady's finger pointing me out...

Madonna of Tenderness, Lady of Feints and Xs, you
      point too.

VIRGINIA REEL

In Clarke County, the story goes, the family name
Was saved by a single crop of wheat,
The houses and land kept in a clear receipt for the
      subsequent suicides,
The hard times and non-believers to qualify and disperse:
Woodburn and Cedar Hall, Smithfield, Auburn and North
      Hill:
Names like white moths kicked up from the tall grass,
Spreading across the countryside
From the Shenandoah to Charles Town and the Blue
      Ridge.

And so it happened. But none of us live here now, in any
      of them,
Though Aunt Roberta is still in town,
Close to the place my great-great-grandfather taught
      Nelly Custis's children once
Answers to Luther. And Cardinal Newman too.
Who cares? Well, I do. It's worth my sighs
To walk here, on the wrong road, tracking a picture back
To its bricks and its point of view.
It's worth my while to be here, crumbling this dirt
      through my bare hands.

I've come back for the first time in 20 years,
Sand in my shoes, my pockets full of the same wind
That brought me before, my flesh
Remiss in the promises it made then, the absolutes it's
      heir to.
This is the road they drove on. And this is the rise
Their blood repaired to, removing its gloves.
And this is the dirt their lives were made of, the dirt the
      world is,
Immeasurable emptiness of all things.

I stand on the porch of Wickliffe Church,
My kinfolk out back in the bee-stitched vines and weeds,
The night coming on, my flat shirt drawing the light in,
Bright bud on the branch of nothing's tree.
In the new shadows, memory starts to shake out its dark
    cloth.
Everyone settles down, transparent and animate,
Under the oak trees.
Hampton passes the wine around, Jaq toasts to our
    health.

And when, from the blear and glittering air,
A hand touches my shoulder,
I want to fall to my knees, and keep on falling, here,
Laid down by the articles that bear my names,
The limestone and marble and locust wood.
But that's for another life. Just down the road, at
    Smithfield, the last of the apple blossom
Fishtails to earth through the shot twilight,
A little vowel for the future, a signal from us to them.

SELF-PORTRAIT

Marostica, Val di Ser. Bassano del Grappa.
Madonna del Ortolo. San Giorgio, arc and stone.
The foothills above the Piave.

Places and things that caught my eye, Walt,
In Italy. On foot, Great Cataloguer, some 20-odd years ago.

San Zeno and Caffe Dante. Catullus' seat.
Lake Garda. The Adige at Ponte Pietra
—I still walk there, a shimmer across the bridge on hot
    days,
The dust, for a little while, lying lightly along my
    sleeve—.
Piazza Erbe, the 12 Apostles...

Over the grave of John Keats
The winter night comes down, her black habit starless
    and edged with ice,
Pure breaths of those who are rising from the dead.

Dino Campana, Arthur Rimbaud.
Hart Crane and Emily Dickinson. The Black Chateau.

CALLED BACK

Friday arrives with all its attendant ecstasies.
Mirrors bloom in the hushed beds.

The ocotillo begins to publish its orange tongues
Down in Sonora, the cactus puts on its beads.
Juan Quezada's Angel of Death, socket and marrow bone,
Stares from its cage and scorched eyes.

I've made my overtures to the Black Dog, and backed off.
I've touched the links in its gold chain.
I've called out and bent down and even acknowledged my
    own face.

Darkness, O Father of Charity, lay on your hands.

For over an hour the joy of the mockingbird has altered
    the leaves.
Stealthily, blossoms have settled along the
    bougainvillaea like purple moths
Catching their breaths, the sky still warm to the touch.
Nothing descends like snow or stiff wings
Out of the night.
        Only the dew falls, soft as the footsteps of the dead.

Language can do just so much,
                    a flurry of damp prayers,
A chatter of glass beside the road's edge,
Flash and a half-glint as the headlights pass...

When the oak tree and the Easter grass have taken my
    body,
I'll start to count out my days, beginning at 1.

SELF-PORTRAIT

In Murray, Kentucky I lay once
On my side, the ghost-weight of a past life in my arms,
A life not mine. I know she was there,
Asking for nothing, heavy as bad luck, still waiting to
    rise.
I know now and I lift her.

Evening becomes us.
I see myself in a tight dissolve, and answer to no one.
Self-traitor, I smuggle in
The spider love, undoer and rearranger of all things.
Angel of Mercy, strip me down.

This world is a little place,
Just red in the sky before the sun rises.
Hold hands, hold hands
That when the birds start, none of us is missing.
Hold hands, hold hands.

Interview

*In the fall of 1977 an in-depth interview with Charles Wright
was published in* **Field** *Number 17. Rather than attempting
to duplicate those efforts, the editor and Charles Wright
agreed that the* **Field** *interview would serve as a point of
departure, that we would move toward new ground. With
that in mind I provided several questions by mail, to which
the poet responded in writing.*

**Q: How has translating—particularly Montale—
affected your own work? What writers outside of the
English language, both contemporary and otherwise,
are you fond of and/or have influenced your work?**

Wright: The translations I did of Pavese, Pasolini and Elio
Pagliarani had no affect on my own work at all, all three of
them writing a more discursive poetry than I was interested
in at the time, or am now. Pavese has a lot to teach anyone,
however, at least through William Arrowsmith's brilliant
versions which are, I think, more interesting in English than
they were in Italian, they sounding so Hemingwayesque in
Italian (a writer Pavese translated into Italian). Montale, of
course, is a different story. There was always some thread in
Montale's work that was tied to my sensibility and every
poem tugged on it to one degree or another. What was
fortunate for me was that I began to translate him at the
same time I began to write poems seriously. Mark Strand
was the first person to encourage me to try my hand at
translating, back in 1961, saying it was a good thing to do
when you were 'between poems.' I thought it was true then
and I still do. After I had been in graduate school for two
years, I got a Fulbright grant to go back to Italy (I had been
there for three years in the Army) to work on Montale,
Pavese and Pasolini. It came at a very good time for me, as I
had spent two very intense years trying to get surfaces to

33

work or beginning to understand what the surface of a poem was about and now I had the chance to see what the insides were about, as I spent the next two years, 1963-65, translating **The Storm & Other Poems** while living in Rome. Translating Montale at such a formative time in my own development was a real gift—I was able to see the grooves and dovetailings, the suspensions and stresses and, in general, most of the physical ways he put poems together; I was also able to see how the poems often worked conceptually, spatially and dramatically. Some of this I have been able to take over and assimilate in my own work. A great deal of it I can merely admire at second hand and hope someday to be good enough to be able to do in my own and different way. There was also a certain spiritual quality in the work I admired, and a way of using hard-edged imagery with genuine sentiment, something lacking in Italian poetry since Dante. I also liked the generally large themes he took on, and the way he took them on—clear-eyed and down-to-earth and unapologetically.

I haven't done any serious translating since then, so I have no *pronunciamentos* on the art in general, except to say that what everyone says is true—it's an impossible task. The one who gets the most from a translation is the translator, not the reader. Which is unfortunate for me, as some of my favorite poets, poets whose work I have loved and been changed by, I have read only in translations—Rimbaud, Baudelaire, Trakl, the late T'ang Chinese, Lorca, Attila Jozsef, Mandelstam, Rilke, Vallejo, Neruda (the *Residencias*)...The list could go on, but it makes one realize why Pound wanted to know all those languages...Celan, Campana, St. John of the Cross...

34

Interview

Q: Do you feel as though you are influenced by your American contemporaries? If so, who? If not, can you pinpoint why—do you believe it unhealthy for a poet to read his contemporaries?

Wright: No—regarding your first question—if you mean poets of my own generation. I suppose there is some affinity with the ones I feel closest to—Mark Strand, Charles Simic and James Tate—but someone else would have to say what it is, or what it is not. I don't really feel any mutual influence going on, though. As for the generation before me, as I've said elsewhere, Donald Justice was an early influence on me, as he was my teacher and I was an empty blackboard just waiting to be written on. I still feel fortunate that he had the chalk. Later, I find that W.S. Merwin and I share a certain spiritual affinity, one I also share with Peter Matthiessen, I think, though he is primarily a prose writer. I suppose there are many poets I have picked up a phrase from here, a turn there or an image here and there. This seems inevitable to me if one reads at all and is open to good things. One thinks of the poets one admires and realizes that some burrs have stuck as one passes through their fields on the way to one's own plot of ground. But none of this is very serious down deep, and would not come under the seminal heading of influence, which is a way of *hearing* things, a way of *seeing*, and *seeing through*, things. For that, I think, one has to—in my case—jump two or three generations ahead to get at what was really happening to me in my malleable years. I think of Pound and Crane (Hart) as primary sources and, earlier, Emily Dickinson (and, from England, Father Hopkins). Perhaps even more basic was early country music, and the lifey/deathy/after-deathy themes inherent in the songs, say, of The Carter Family, Roy Acuff, Merle Travis and early Lester Flatt and Earl Scruggs. This is a round-about way of

35

saying that I think one should try to avoid being influenced by one's American contemporaries in any deep sense. One reads them, of course, just as you hope they read you, with appreciation and sometimes great admiration, but there are greater lessons to be learned from the dead than from the living, ultimately, as they have all the secrets.

Q: In the FIELD interview you remarked: "I'm not interested in a flat line, or the flat language that has been fairly popular in the last, say, 10 to 12 years." Could you elaborate on this? It seems to me that this popularity germinates from the erroneous equating of honesty/directness/and clean diction with flatness. How does that strike you? You also mentioned, in the FIELD piece, "I suspect that 'Skins,' and 'Tattoos' as well, is over-written to a certain extent." Could you speak toward pinpointing a middleway between flat language and over-writing?

Wright: I'm not sure how much elaboration is either called for or is possible. As I try to look back on my motives for saying such a thing from the vantage point of today (January 1979; the interview took place in November 1976), it seems likely that they were at least two: one, surely, was because it was so popular and had been used so much and, so often, badly. And, two, since I had worked hard in the opposite field, I felt, I'm sure, some real stake in supporting my own position. And, three, since I hadn't really 'chosen' a more 'musical' line, it coming more or less naturally to me (as I tried to explain in the interview), it seems probable that I felt more evangelical in its defense than I might have otherwise. And, fourth, I guess, I just prefer music to drone, in whatever form it comes. I still feel these ways and, if anything, have an even greater interest in the sound and weight and rub and glint of words.

As for the popularity of the flat line, I think you're probably correct in your reasons for its popularity. It also, I might add, seems so easy to write. In this it's like free verse, which seems so easy to do, and is, but is so difficult to do well.

And as for "Skins" and "Tatoos" being over-written, if I really felt that at the time (which I doubt; it sounds like a very defensive statement to me), I no longer believe it. They both got, I hope, the closest I could come at the time to the rhythms and rhetoric I thought they needed. And I look at them now—even though I probably wouldn't write them again in exactly the same way—as a middle way, given their subject matter and my leanings, between a flat style and one that is over-written and excessive.

Q: Speaking of CHINA TRACE in the FIELD interview, you remarked: "I'm trying to talk about things that I don't know anything about, because I haven't been there, in terms of something I do know something about, because I'm standing in the middle of them." I'm wondering if the antithesis of this statement could not as well apply to the book, if someone couldn't make a case for the opposite: that you found a form of projecting, for objectification, certain subject matter onto this China trace, and came to understand the things you were "standing in the middle of" via this new perspective. It's a weird epistemological problem—the particular is cast out on the general, the abstract, for form (as Plato would have it), and then retrieved and dealt with in a certain context. What do you think?

Wright: I think we should break for lunch. But before we do,

I'd say you could certainly do it that way, as the main thing is to understand the things one is "standing in the middle of"—one's life and how one lives it. Writing poems should have to do with helping you live and understand your life. Your poems should help you to understand yourself and the world around you, no? Your poems should, if you work hard enough at them, help you to come to terms with whatever there is, wherever it is. They perhaps won't solve anything (although often they might), but they should at least ease your passage from one place to the next. Poems are both reliquary and transubstantiational, as our lives should be.

Q: Are you interested in speaking further re the use of the line, the use of the page's white space (the doughnut hole, as Mandelstam called it) and/or your counting of stresses and syllables?

Wright: The white space is really white sound (the technical term is 'white noise'), sound the ear doesn't always pick up but which is always there, humming, backgrounding, like silences. It's what pulls the lines through the poem, gauging their weights and durations, even their distances. It is the larger sound out of which the more measured and interruptable sounds of the line are cut. And it is always there, the faint hissing that tells us where to go and where to avoid.

The line, of course, is what separates us from the beasts. I think a line has specific weight and heft, that it is melodic and tactile. It is as though the lines were each sections of the poem attached by invisible strings to the title, the way the various parts of a marionette are attached by strings to the control board. Each line exists in itself as each separate part of the marionette exists independently and interdependently. It is only when the strings are all being used in unison from the board that the marionette operates properly. The same with lines/poem/title. Lines have movements, turns and meanings independent of the poem as a whole, etc., etc....

I don't count stresses and syllables quite as assiduously as I did a couple of years ago. I still count them, but more after the fact, to confirm my ear rather than to guide and control it. I still like to know exactly what's there, and if a rhythmic repetition is done on purpose or has happened by unfortunate accident. It's just something I do, and has no theoretical value other than contributing to the weight and duration of the line itself. And the line, as we all know, and as I've just repeated, is the linchpin of the poem. Without it, the wheels come off. With badly made ones, the entire vehicle moves awkwardly. Weak ones snap.

Q: Could you speak about the poems printed in the PROFILE in their relation to the trilogy? When the trilogy, after many years work, was completed, you were no doubt confronted with aesthetic decisions— can you address yourself to these decisions and their manifestations as presented in the PROFILE?

Wright: Rather than a "trilogy," I prefer to think of the books as a triptych, three different and separate instances in the same life instead of the linkage that the literary term "trilogy" seems to carry. It may be nit-picking, but I don't see the books as inter-related as a "trilogy" signifies. The linkage is my life, not any superimposition that the books posit. Mantegna's triptych of Christ in Perugia is of three separate ages in his life, and uses three discrete panels. In my case the panels are yesterday, today and tomorrow. Somehow, looking at the books in this way makes a difference: they stand as individual books, but are on the same background, in the same frame. One doesn't need the others, but all are informed by each other.

As for the **Profile** poems, their relationship to **Hard Freight**, **Bloodlines** and **China Trace** in minimal, if even extant. "Homage to Paul Cezanne" has an energy runover from **China Trace**, but that's all. There may be some autobiographical tie-in in the odd poem, but that's unintentional and inevitable. I am trying to make what I'm working on now as little like what I did before as my style and subject matter will allow. Since I write out of obsessions, I don't know how far away this will be, but I hope it's far enough. There are, of course, technical follow-throughs and extensions in the ten poems here, especially from **China Trace**. I was trying for a perhaps unreachable compression in the **China Trace** line and stanza. One of the technical considerations I'm interested in in these new poems is an attempt to put the heavily freighted and compressed, synaptically-linked line into a more expanded context, i.e., longer lines and longer poems. I'm also still very involved with making the stanza a unit of measure (Hopkins and Williams both did this, in differing ways; and others, too, I suppose) the way certain color constructions become focal points in paintings.

Q: In the FIELD interview you mentioned the hope of writing, after completion of CHINA TRACE, a long poem which would attempt to translate a painter's technique to the page. Is "Homage to Paul Cezanne" that poem? If so, could you elaborate on this technique? Could you offer anything else about the poem that might be of help or interest?

Wright: It is, indeed, the poem, although 'painter's

40

technique' is surely too inclusive a term. How it comes closest is in its non-linear approach to plot. Which is to say that I doubt you could 'plot' the poem if you were of a mind to do so. The structure of the poem is presentational, and it works accumulatively. Which, again, is to say that it works in layers or overlays, much as a painting would do, until it has reached completion. The sections aren't haphazard or substitutable, however, any more than certain layers or brushstrokes or colors are. They go in the order they have, which is, I hope, an accumulative order, but they are not numbered, hence they are not sections as we usually understand them in poems. As far as other painterly techniques are concerned, I was conscious of working in blocks of lines, stanzas and pages, much as Cezanne might have used his dabs and columns and blotches of color (in many of the Mt. St. Victoire landscapes you can't find a line at all—everything is dab and spread and knife-stroke and, in the finished painting, extremely representational). The poem as painting, etc., visualization of abstracts, filling in the corners...

I deliberately chose an abstract subject matter (the Dead) that was as close to a tactile and animate one as I could come up with. It made the theoretical possibilities (i.e., language for paint) more plastic and malleable. The poem has nothing to do with him as a man, and everything to do with him as a painter, the way he painted in the last 20-30 years of his life. The poem began as a technical experiment and rapidly (after the first page) became something much more. As is the case in most anything you do that you eventually value, what you say becomes so much more important than how you say it. And that aspect of the poem will have to speak for itself. As for the so-called 'painter's technique', I had used it in parts of **Bloodlines** and to a real extent in **China Trace**. I am now doing it even more extensively in this 'book.' As I say, 'painter's technique' is, I believe, inaccurate for the most part. And whatever it is I'm doing will have to wait for its term, if it deserves one.

Q: In the poem "12 Lines at Midnight" there is a line 'The breath inside my breath is the breath of the dream.' I sense, from this line and the FIELD interview, a sense of both 'you are what you are going to be' and that you're not, that, as many writers are, you are motivated by imperfection, a strive toward something greater, toward saying It in perfection once and for all, toward over-stepping—as Nietzsche would put it—yourself. On the one hand, as soon as you say It you're doomed, because there's nothing beyond It but silence; on the other hand, there seems to be the horrible truth that language can never accomplish It, cannot communicate—cannot function—in these quintessential spheres. To bring this to a less theoretical issue, Faulkner commented, 'Always dream and shoot higher than you know you can do. Don't bother just to be better than your contemporaries or predecessors. Try to be better than yourself.' Can you respond, somehow, to this?

Wright: Well, you've just given the answers. What, as Gertrude Stein said, is the question? I do think you're correct in the first two sentences, but one out of two in the third one. Certainly I am guilty of sentence #2 (and #1), although it is a guilt I wear with a certain amount of vanity. The first half of the third sentence I think is wrong because of the word 'doomed.' If you ever said It, you'd be saved, not doomed. And what a glorious silence! I am becoming more and more aware of the truth of the second half of the third sentence, and I mention that awareness twice in poems in this **Profile.**

And, of course, Faulkner is right. Still, as Homer knew, and others after him, what's important is the journey itself. My true Penelope is Penelope.

Q: Could you speak about your use of the self-portrait (which seems to be almost a sharper focus on your use of autobiographical material in general)?

Wright: In general, I think it's true that these five self-portraits are more autobiographical than descriptive. They stand as a model in miniature of a process I am trying to bring across in the entire body of the projected 'book' I'm working on, and which the ten poems in the **Profile** form, or will form, the first two sections of.

Francis Bacon has done series of self-portraits (3-4 in a series) in which the image is broken down and distorted a little more in each succeeding picture, all the while retaining the central focus and outline of the picture as a whole and as a composite. If brushstrokes and brushwork can be equated, in this case, with language, and form can still be considered form, then I'm after something like this. And not merely for oddity's sake, but as a further step in trying to understand the elasticity, availability and ultimate desirability of language as a means.

The first two self-portraits I did (one in **The Grave of the Right Hand** and one in **Hard Freight**—"Portrait of the Poet in Abraham von Werdt's Dream") were purely technical exercises. The third (in **China Trace**) was more serious, and these five, even though originally technically oriented, have come to be the most serious of all, in that I hope they say something about my life, and how I look at it. The second and third ones in the **Profile** group are made up, for the most part, from postcards and photographs that are above my desk. Four has to do with my years in Italy, and five uses rearranged material, in part, from John Donne and Emily Dickinson. All five are separated and punctuated by four longer poems about rebirth, and all nine poems are supposed to work together in the movement of the Bacon paintings. "Called Back," for instance, is supposed to be the least narratively inclined of all the nine poems, each section being more or less independent. The same goes for the last self-portrait. Finally, of course, the poems have no referents but the language, as they have nothing to do contextually with anyone's paintings. They have to do, as I say, with my life, and where and how I live it.

Q: Do you, as many poets do, keep a journal?

Wright: No, but I do keep, off and on, or have kept off and on over the past year or so, a sort of "commonplace notebook" where I jot down quotes or thoughts of my own that I happen to cotton to at the moment. What follows is most of the notebook, so you can see that it hasn't been extensive or obsessive.

A Pound (and Whitman) Sampler:
—The unseen is proved by the seen, which in its turn becomes the unseen and is proved.
—The image is the poet's pigment.
—The vortex is the point of maximum energy.
—Every emotion has its rhythm.
—Symbols have a fixed value, as 1, 2, 7 in arithmetic. Images have a variable significance, as a, b or x in algebra.
—A symbol is a permanent metaphor.
—An image is an intellectual and emotional complex in a given instant.
—The image records the instant when an outward and objective thing is transformed to a thing inward and

subjective.

"The outward and visible sigh of an inward and spiritual grace."

"A place belongs forever to whoever claims it hardest, remembers it most obsessively, wrenches it from itself, shapes it, renders it, loves it so radically that he remakes it in his image..."
—Joan Didion on James Jones

Two new lines for "Holy Thursday." The 'fly jump' in the second stanza is a warning shot, a tracer...

People keep saying, Life is like war. Life is not like war, life is like summer camp.

Never break into lines and try to pass off as a poem something you would be embarrassed to write down in prose.

"Cezanne: 'I have my motif...' (He joins his hands.)
Gasquet: 'What?'
Cezanne: 'Yes...' (He repeats his gesture, spreads his hands, the ten fingers open, brings them together slowly, slowly, then joins them, squeezes them, clenches them, inserts them together.) 'There's what must be attained...There must not be a single link too loose, a hole through which the emotion, the light or the truth may escape. I advance my entire picture at one time, you understand...I bring together in the same spirit, the same faith, all that is scattered...I take from right, from left, from here, there, everywhere, tones, colors, shades; I fix them; I bring them together...My canvas joins hands. It does not vacillate.'"
—(J. Gasquet, **Cezanne**, Paris, 1921, p. 80,

45

based on a translation by Lawrence Gowing...)

"A little glimpse of death, and the looseness and tolerance that brings."
—Allen Ginsberg on what he 'needs' to write

Rimbaud, Trakl and Hart Crane: 3 favorites. It's their passion I love. They are great 'I' poets, whatever persona they use.

"The great ones always speak from the other side."
—Leonard Michaels

"...the symbolic imagination...a dramatic imagination in the sense that its fullest image is an action in the shapes of this world: it does not reject, it includes: it sees not only with, but through, the natural world to what may lie beyond it."
—Allen Tate

A painting is occupying (inhabiting) a given space in front of you. A poem is the same thing.

"...he defined himself as a supporter of 'Western liberal democracy, favouring an intellectual elite and a progressive middle class and based on a moral order derived from Christian absolutes."
—Tom Stoppard

"There is a kind of cleanness and virginity in it, in this looking away from oneself; it is as though one were drawing, one's gaze bound to the object, inwoven with Nature, while one's hand goes its own way somewhere below, goes on and on, gets timid, wavers, is glad again, goes on and on far

Interview

below the face that stands like a star above it, not looking,
only shining. I feel as though I had always worked that way;
face gazing at far things, hands alone. And so it surely ought
to be. I shall be like that again in time."

—Rilke

"My business is circumference."   —Emily Dickinson

"The move toward a disintegration of the object in some of
the most memorable works of a painter so passionately
attached to objects is the attraction and the riddle of
Cezanne's last phase. The element that usurped its place, the
patch of color in itself..."

—Gowing on Cezanne

The object is the poem, the patch of color is the stanza (the
line?).

A Japanese student in America quoted in Pound's **ABC of
Reading** on the difference between prose and poetry:
"Poetry consists of gists and piths."

"Night be good, do not let me die."

—Apache invocation

The primary level of the poem is bread mold. The secondary
meaning, the resonance, is the mystery that heals, the
penicillin.

Imagistic tone of voice
Imagistic structure

Narrative tone of voice
Narrative structure

———————

Hard Freight: imagistic tone, narrative structure
Bloodlines: all 4
China Trace: imagistic structure
narrative tone

"The recourse to talent shows a defect in the imagination."
—Georges Braque

The rhetorical silences in the long, image-freighted line—the rhetoric of silence...(from "Cezanne..." on)

Pure technique is the spider web without the spider—it glitters and catches but it doesn't kill.

Poems should come out of the body, like webbing from the spider.

"Momentous depths of speculation." —Keats

For M., who wants 'eyesight, not vision'—There's more to poetry than meets the eye (see Crane's comment on 'retinal registration.')

Art tends toward the certainty of making connections. The artist's job is to keep things apart, allowing the synapses to speak.

When the finger of God appears, it's usually the wrong finger.

Interview

Language is always the big winner in pot limit poetry. And pot limit is the only real game in town.

The best narrative is that which is least in evidence to the eye.

"The ultimate fate and duty of the poet is visionary..."
—Denis Donoghue

"Transform? Yes; for our task is so deeply and so passionately to impress upon ourselves this provisional and perishable earth, that its essential being will rise again 'invisibly' in us. *We are the bees of the invisible. We frantically plunder the visible of its honey, to accumulate it in the great golden hive of the invisible.*"
—Rilke

The Poetry of
Charles Wright

I.

China Trace, Charles Wright's fourth book of poems, completes the trilogy begun with **Hard Freight**, Wright's second book, and continued through his much praised third collection, **Bloodlines**. It seemed natural that, after the finely crafted, visually acute and precise poems of his first volume, **The Grave of the Right Hand**, Wright should feel the need to gather his past, to in some sense write—and rewrite—not only that past, but also the self, the poetic self and voice, which he was bringing to his newer and more ambitious poems. In terms of style, it was the poem "Dog Creek Mainline," from **Hard Freight**, which first signalled this new direction for Wright. Knotty, rhythmically muscular, alliterative, and still highly imagistic and visual, the poetry took on a beautiful rasping quality, reflecting not only the abstract concerns and music behind the language, but revealing in the choices of auto-biographical subjects what would become a central impulse and recurring theme in Wright's work.

In **Hard Freight** and **Bloodlines** familial memories and episodes of Wright's youth in Tennessee and North Carolina mix easily with the natural landscapes of their settings. Then, in **Bloodlines**, Wright begins the process of not only attempting to orient himself to the past, now as a mature speaker, but to orient himself in relation to his own *present* and *presence* as well. The book revolves around two long sequences, "Tattoos" and "Skins," each of the poems consisting of twenty parts, each serving to echo the concerns of the other. "Tatoos" illustrates a list of psychologically potent events which have each in some way marked Wright. "Skins" is a highly abstract inquiry into the materials of existence, the most elemental as well as the most metaphysical. The poem's philosophical issues combine in what becomes a verbal, intellectual music; primal images and his everpresent anxieties about death riddle the sequence as Wright attempts not only to lay to rest his reclamation of the past (and to answer his own mistrusts while ordering his present), but to look toward the certain—if ill-defined—terrain of his future as well. This terrain, of course, takes as its horizon Wright's death. Though, in **China Trace**, Wright will ask what may exist (albeit only in his own yearnings and imaginings) beyond that horizon, it is in **Bloodlines**, at the end of the final section of "Skins," that the meditations found in **China Trace** really begin:

> And what does it come to, Pilgrim,
> This walking to and fro on the earth, knowing
> That nothing changes, or everything;
> And only, to tell it, these sad marks,
> Phrases half-parsed, ellipses and scratches across the dirt?
> It comes to a point. It comes and it goes.

So, it is with these "sad marks" that Wright begins his attempt to tell not only wht it comes to, but where—and why—it goes beyond.

China Trace is a unique book. None of its poems are longer than twelve lines. The book is divided into two sections, each section made up of twenty-five poems, each section bearing the identical epigraph from Italo Calvino's **Invisible Cities**: "On the day when I know all the emblems," Kublai Khan asked Marco, "shall I be able to possess my empire, at last?" And the Venetian answered:

54

"Sire, do not believe it. On that day you will be an emblem among emblems."

China Trace is a personal history pushed toward its future; the speaker reaches toward his own death and the desired salvation it may or may not bring. Wright often, in the course of the book, clearly does *not* believe, yet he feels called upon to continue the search his yearnings have prompted. The book is filled with portents of what's to come, as in the poems "Next" (I want to lie down, I am so tired, and let/ The crab grass seep through my heart,/ Side by side with the inchworm and the fallen psalm,/ Close to the river bank,/ In autumn, the red leaves in the sky/ Like lost flags, sidle and drift...") and "January" (In some other life/ I'll stand where I'm standing now, and will look down, and will see/ My own face, and not know what I'm looking at). Again, as in the poem "Skins," it is the elemental regeneration of a life, its death into decay, the body passing through its cycle of water, earth, fire, and air, which is the most one might ask for as salvation. Here in "Self-Portrait in 2035" is Wright imagining himself at 100 years old:

> The root becomes him, the road ruts
> That are sift and grain in the powderlight
> Recast him, sink bone in him,
> Blanket and creep up, fine, fine;
>
> Worm-waste and pillow tick; hair
> Prickly and dust-dangled, his arms and black shoes
> Unlinked and laceless, his face false
> In the wood-rot, and past pause...
>
> Darkness, erase these lines, forget these words.
> Spider recite his one sin.

China Trace is full of small cosmologies posited by Wright as approximations of what is and what's to come.

Even if, as he says in the poem "Morandi" (for the Italian painter), it is "the void/ These objects sentry for, and rise from" it is clear that **China Trace** is firmly rooted in those objects of daily life, in the earth, the domestic experience reflected in the journal-like quality of many of the poems. It is no accident the poems are often fixed not only by place names, but by specific times of day or night, phases of the moon, dates, and personal references as well. In this diary of passage, the natural and ordinary must balance what otherwise could seem the illusions all dreamers must perform. Thus, it remains vital to Wright that he continuously mark or notate his search with the facts of his existence, otherwise what point would such a search have?

Though often seeming alternately impressionistic and expressionistic in its impact, **China Trace** carries the clarity of dramatic narrative and a formal precision throughout. The poems function as a sequence, as a long meditation. It is a soul's search for salvation; a man's fixed being on the earth and his yearning for the *other*. Wright has said **China Trace** might be called "A Book of Yearning." Detailing his ambitious, cosmic reachings with the ordinary and the daily, Wright continues to look outward. Here, for example, is "Clear Night":

Clear night, thumb-top of a moon, a back-lit sky.
Moon-fingers lay down their same routine
On the side deck and the threshold, the white keys
    and the black keys.
Bird hush and bird song. A cassia flower falls.

I want to be bruised by God.
I want to be strung up in a strong light and singled out.
I want to be stretched, like music wrung from a dropped seed.
I want to be entered and picked clean.

56

And the wind says "What?" to me.
And the castor beans, with their little earrings of
　　death, say "What?" to me.
And the stars start out on their cold slide through the dark.
And the gears notch and the engines wheel.

China Trace is a pilgrim's book, the same "Pilgrim"
addressed at the conclusion of "Skins." It is a guidebook of
spiritual passage, with nods to fellow travellers along the
way. Though Wright has little of Merwin's "icy" tone, as he
is far too lush a poet, he is still able to echo a quality of voice
we find in Merwin, that of a speaker who has suffered his
own silence, in seclusion, for a long while; a speaker who has
walked off from the tribe, the city, in order to turn and, at
last, speak to and for it. In "Depression Before the Solstice"
Wright sees:

　The watchers and holy ones set out, divining the seal, eclipses
　Taped to their sleeves with black felt,
　Their footsteps filling with sparks
　In the bitter loam behind them, ahead of them stobbed with sand,
　And walk hard, and regret nothing.

There is often a hermetic tone to **China Trace**, perhaps
reflecting the influence of Montale, whom Wright has
translated so well. In the illuminating *instants* of **China
Trace** we are in the presence—as in the finest of religious
works—of the mystery of the *one*, the individual, confronted
by the expanse of the greater and more fluent *other*. From
"Stone Canyon Nocturne":

　Ancient of Days, old friend, no one believes you'll come back.
　No one believes in his own life anymore.

57

> The moon, like a dead heart, cold and unstartable, hangs
> > by a thread
> At the earth's edge,
> Unfaithful at last, splotching the ferns and the pink shrubs.
>
> In the other world, children undo the knots in their tally strings.
> They sing songs, and their fingers blear.
>
> And here, where the swan hums in his socket, where bloodroot
> And belladonna insist on our comforting,
> Where the fox in the canyon wall empties our hands, ecstatic for
> > more,
>
> Like a bead of clear oil the Healer revolves through the night
> > wind,
> Part eye, part tear, unwilling to recognize us.

It is the proper relationship to what "lies beyond" that Wright is trying to explore, fear and acquiescence both being inadequate. There is something in Wright's spirituality which reminds me of Ginsberg or Kerouac at their best, which is to say their least extravagant. The attempt to weld an Eastern conscience with a Western sensibility, which has led others only to self-absorption, ecstatic or otherwise, leads Wright back to *language*, which is, for all of our best poets, the root of the desire to search with and within speech.

For Wright, this search has acquired a more heightened and extremely graphic sense of language. Wright is almost painterly in his notion of word play and his execution of often dazzling verbal chromatics. It is as if Wright's poems keep seeking some ideogramatic form, and as such exist almost as another language, somewhere between the language we know and the glyphs of an obscure, ritualistic cult. There is much the tone of Yeats' occult clarity and Rilke's sonorous passion in these poems. Often the natural elements themselves appear in the act of "writing" themselves across the face of the earth or sky. It is the

David St. John

physical signature of passage, both man's and the world's, which intrigues Wright. Yet, what gives the poems their unique presence is Wright's love and admiration for Pound. It has driven Wright to nearly create another tongue, not so much to "make it new" as to allow for certain liberties in his poems. Wright seeks to carry in the poems the best of the physical and visual complexities of a sign-language, a graphic poetics, while still absorbing what he finds to be the most sensuous and aural flavors of English. Wright is not above coining words, and he delights in alliterative bursts and eccentric—and memorable—word combinations, as well as compressed constructions for the poems themselves.

It would seem easy to cite Hopkins in talking about **China Trace**, but finally one feels Hopkins influence really quite marginally. It is Wright responding to a tremendous *internal* pressure himself—to find the proper word construct, the right syllable mobile, the most pleasing sound ladder, all of which must correctly convey his anxious, metaphysical explorations.

There is clearly a risk of this notion of language coupled with so demanding a subject, but Wright is an impeccable stylist, and he remains firm about the importance of the personal details attending the poems. They remain for all of us rooted in experience while seeking some greater more universal equation.

The book "traces" these grand passions, then, with Wright's precise notation, with his compressed imagistic clarity. If we wonder where the road of these poems can possibly end, it is the end we knew had to be reached from the beginning. If we wonder what will become of the "Pilgrim" who has disguised himself in this book so often as "I," "You," and "He," then we are answered in the final poem of **China Trace**, "Him":

59

His sorrow hangs like a heart in the star-flowered boundary tree.
It mirrors the endless wind.

He feeds on the lunar differences and flies up at the dawn.

When he lies down, the waters will lie down with him,
And all that walks and all that stands still, and sleeps
          through the thunder.

It's for him that the willow bleeds.

Look for him high in the flat black of the northern Pacific sky,
Released in his suit of lights,
                              lifted and laid clear.

II.

    One of the most striking aspects of Charles Wright's new
poems, the poems written since **China Trace** and collected
for this **Profile**, is that they remain, like the poems of **China
Trace**, resolutely spiritual in their character. They are
devotional while yet being constantly worldly; these poems
are considerations of the life of the spirit. By "spirit" we
mean that motivating vitality within a life, as well as that
supernatural entity which, after its presence on earth, finds
its residence in some other unnameable, yet congruent,
realm. Charles Wright's meditations and verbal
iconographies force us to consider that most unfashionable
of topics: the soul. It is his commitment to this most difficult
of subjects which, when coupled with his technical finesse,

David St. John

makes Wright's poetry unique among contemporary works. Not surprisingly, we find that these poems encompass what we would call ideas of faith, of belief. Yet, in all of Wright's work, we find that he is engaged in a struggle with all that is doctrinaire in our conceptions of what is "faith" and "belief." Wright's own faiths rest always upon the possibility (and hope) of naming in his poetry—though never facilely or with the slightest arrogance of certitude— that region of intersection between this life and any other. It is in this region that both the spirit of the living and the spirits of the dead will, if anywhere, mingle. It is Wright's attempt to describe for us the geography of this rarely traveled terrain, its purgatorial wastes and paradisal instants, which sustains for a reader the fascination of his work. Again, it is important to remember that Wright's notations in the log remain heroically concrete, even domestically personal and self-revealing. Furthermore, Wright maps our way with both humor and tenderness. Always, it is Wright's intricate clarity, the precision of his ambitious imagistic equations, which illuminates and holds us to his difficult landscapes. There is no question that Wright can be a demanding poet. Often, we find ourselves within or confronted by a sequence of rhythmic imperatives, all propelling an abstract or complex passage. In these instances, however, Wright's demands upon us end in the reward of a more wholly realized and more finely imagined matrix of emotion. Wright continually searches beyond any inadequacy of our language, that he might be more exacting and inventive in his phrasings, so that each poem resonates more clearly with the details of his experience as well as with the subtleties of his chromatically constructed metaphors.

If we look, for example, to the fourth section of Wright's stunning poem, "Homage to Paul Cezanne," we find that he has taken that precise yet diffusely abstract term "the dead" as the literal material of his landscape building (making). We find that, in the creation of this landscape, the painterly terms one might use to describe Cezanne's process of landscape painting (building) have been transposed to the poem in such a way that they have been appropriated into the idea and the subject/substance of the materials, "the dead." Here is that fourth section:

The dead are a cadmium blue.
We spread them with palette knives in broad blocks and planes.

We layer them stroke by stroke
In steps and ascending mass, in verticals raised from the earth.

We choose, and layer them in,
Blue and a blue and a breath,

Circle and smudge, cross-beak and button hook,
We layer them in. We squint hard and terrace them line by line.

And so we are come between, and cry out,
And stare up at the sky and its cloudy panes,

And finger the cypress twists.
The dead understand all this, and keep in touch,

Rustle of hand to hand in the lemon trees,
Flags, and the great sifts of anger

To powder and nothingness.
The dead are a cadmium blue, and they understand.

In section six of "Homage to Paul Cezanne" we come upon a true split of body and soul. Yet, the spirit's objectification here is hardly terrifying. The self of the spirit rises from the self of the body, and watches the latter, caught between the world of other "spirits" and the physicality of its own body. The spirit hovers, then returns (temporarily) to its physical

62

form. The importance of this episode is that it is of the quality of self-examination and self-reflection which occurs throughout Charles Wright's new poems. Also, this section exists as the counterpoint to the line, reflecting perhaps what is often the temporal condition of Wright's poems, which stands at the beginning of the last section of "Homage to Paul Cezanne": "We're out here, our feet in the soil, our heads craned up at the sky...."

In Wright's series of "Self-Portrait" poems, we find again that quality of self-objectification found in section six of "Homage to Paul Cezanne." In these "Self-Portrait" poems, aspects of self-consideration and self-reflection dominate each poem, calling up the personal details necessary to explore further Wright's notions of self-disintegration and rebirth. These aspects and details exist as elements isolated from a life, from a past. For example, there are the "Self-Portrait" poems which take items and descriptions from real photographs or postcards pinned to the wall of Wright's study in California. Once again, the spirit is observing its own body, its place in the physical world, all the while measuring for itself the speed with which that place in the world is moving toward an inevitable end. This also reflects Wright's view that these "Self-Portrait" poems in some ways echo or emulate Francis Bacon's self-portrait paintings, in that they are progressively more "broken down and distorted" while retaining essentially the same (self) composite. All of Wright's poems seek to discuss the ways in which the physicality of life (of a life) is perpetually in the process of being dispersed both by and through (out) the elemental gnashings of the earth. Finally, of course, it is those figurative and literal winds which will "spirit" that life away. As Wright's final "Self-Portrait" becomes clearly the portrait of a visitation, we find that both the speaker and the attendant presence merge to define that which is, at the end, the One.

In another of Wright's recent poems, "Mount Caribou At Night," we come upon a more specific and literal landscape of the dead. What strikes us in this graveyard scene is the sense of its almost timeless coordinates, its echo of generation and regeneration. In "Virginia Reel" there is this same echo (as there is in earlier of Wright's poems, especially in the book **Hard Freight**), the same reverential reckoning of the familial legacy left in a life. In "Virginia Reel" these generations partake in the process of self-regeneration, serving both as the context and the landscape against which the speaker, the self, moves. It is here that we discover again Wright's constant impulse towards harmony with the elements of his past, his daily present, and his reeling future.

Returning for a moment to the fourth of Wright's "Self-Portrait" poems, we find another aspect of this search for harmony. In this poem, in the context of his years spent in Italy, Wright lists those other presences—outside of his family—with whom he feels a fierce relatedness. He names several dead poets he recognizes, in that mirror the dead drag with them, as precursive images of the self he *would be*. It is with the voices of these poets, then, that Wright seeks the harmony of his own voice, his own poems. Also, it is no accident that, elsewhere, Wright mentions his closeness to American country music, to the songs of artists like The Carter Family. The character and urgency of those songs run throughout many of Wright's poems. Perhaps those special harmonies which made The Carter Family so distinctive are not unrelated to the harmonies we find reading the work of the poets mentioned at the end of the fourth "Self-Portrait" in conjunction with these recent poems of Charles Wright's. There is something aurally illuminating and spiritually moving about them both.

It remains clear to us, in these new poems, that Wright is

David St. John

yet concerned with the *materials* of language, with
exploring the malleability of those materials, perhaps more
than any poet now writing. There is always a tactile and
visual consciousness at work in these poems, one which
insures a three-dimensional illusion within even the most
abstract of the poems. Finally, we must see that Wright has
given us, in the poems since **China Trace**, a more complete
exposure of both his world-view and his self-view. While the
whole notion of self-portrait is necessarily narcissistic,
Charles Wright has exploited this device to make it work
toward a generosity of spirit. Wright has opened up the self-
considerations in his poetry to include the world of the
living, in which his readers and he must continue to comfort
one another for the moment, and the world of the spirit,
which everywhere, as in these poems, breathes around us.

—David St. John

Charles Wright

Charles Wright was born in 1935 in Pickwick Dam, Hardin County, Tennessee, and grew up in Tennessee and North Carolina. He attended Davidson College, The University of Iowa and The University of Rome. From 1957-61 he was in the Army Intelligence Service, stationed for most of this time in Verona, Italy. In 1963-65 he was a Fulbright Student in Rome, translating the poems of the Italian poets Eugenio Montale and Cesare Pavese. In 1968-69 he was a Fulbright Lecturer in North American Literature at the University of Padua. Since 1966 he has been a member of the English Department of the University of California, Irvine. He was a recipient of a National Endowment for the Arts Award in 1974 and a Guggenheim Fellowship in Poetry for 1975-76. In 1969 he was awarded the Eunice Tietjens Award by Poetry Magazine and, in 1976, the Melville Cane Award from The Poetry Society of America. Also in 1976 The Academy of American Poets gave him its Edgar Allan Poe Award. In 1977 The American Academy and Institute of Arts & Letters awarded him one of its Academy-Institute Grants. He has taught, in a visiting capacity, at the University of Iowa, Columbia University and Princeton University. He lives in Laguna Beach, California, with his wife, the photographer Holly Wright, and son, Luke.

Select Bibliography

BOOKS

THE GRAVE OF THE RIGHT HAND, 1970, Wesleyan University Press
HARD FREIGHT, 1973, Wesleyan University Press
BLOODLINES, 1975, Wesleyan University Press
CHINA TRACE, 1977, Wesleyan University Press

CHAPBOOKS

THE DREAM ANIMAL, 1968, House of Anansi Press, Toronto
THE VENICE NOTEBOOK, 1971, Barn Dream Press, Boston
COLOPHONS, 1977, The Windhover Press, Iowa City

PAMPHLETS

THE VOYAGE, 1963, The Patrician Press, Iowa City
6 POEMS, 1965, David Freed, London
BACKWATER, 1973, The Golem Press, Santa Ana

TRANSLATIONS

THE STORM & OTHER POEMS, Eugenio Montale, 1978, Field, Oberlin, Ohio
THE SELECTED POEMS OF EUGENIO MONTALE, 1965, New Directions*
MODERN EUROPEAN POETRY, 1966, Bantam Books (1 poem by Pier Paolo Pasolini)
Chelsea Magazine #14, January 1964 (15 poems by Eugenio Montale)
Chelsea Magazine #14, January 1964 (5 poems by Cesare Pavese)
Chelsea Magazine #18/19, June 1966 (poems by Elio Pagliarani)
Granite Magazine, 1975, (10 poems by Eugenio Montale)
Pequod Magazine, Winter 1977 (20 poems by Eugenio Montale)

*1 of 15 translators (19 poems)